Emory Washburn

Professional Training as an Element of Success and

Conservative Influence

Emory Washburn

Professional Training as an Element of Success and Conservative Influence

ISBN/EAN: 9783744726702

Printed in Europe, USA, Canada, Australia, Japan

Cover: Foto ©Lupo / pixelio.de

More available books at **www.hansebooks.com**

MORAL AND RELIGIOUS EDUCATION
OF THE WORKING CLASSES.

THE

SPEECH

OF

LORD ASHLEY, M.P.,

IN

THE HOUSE OF COMMONS,

ON TUESDAY, FEBRUARY 28, 1843.

On Moving, "That an Humble Address be presented to her Majesty, pray-
" ing that her Majesty will be graciously pleased to take into her instant and
" serious consideration, the best means of diffusing the benefits and blessings
" of a moral and religious education amongst the working classes of her
" people."

LONDON:

JOHN OLLIVIER, 59, PALL MALL.

1843.

SPEECH.

SIR,—The question, that I have undertaken to submit to the deliberation of this House, is one so prodigiously vast, and so unspeakably important, that there may well be demanded an apology, if not an explanation, from any individual member who presumes to handle so weighty and so difficult a matter. And, Sir, had any real difference of opinion existed, I should probably have refrained from the task; but late events have, I fear, proved that the moral condition of our people is unhealthy and even perilous—all are pretty nearly agreed that something further must be attempted for their welfare; and I now venture, therefore, to offer, for the discussion, both matter and opportunity.

Surely, Sir, it will not be necessary as a preliminary to this motion to enquire on whom should rest the responsibility of our present condition—our duty is to examine the moral state of the country; to say whether it be safe, honourable, happy, and becoming the dignity of a Christian kingdom; and, if it be not so, to address ourselves to the cure of evils which, unlike most inveterate and deeply-rooted abuses, though they cannot be suffered to exist without danger, may be removed without the slightest grievance, real or imaginary, to any community or even any individual.

The present time, too, is so far favourable to the propounding of this question, as that it finds us in a state of mind equally distant, I believe, from the two extremes of opinion; the one, that education is the direct, immediate, and lasting panacea for all our disorders; the other, that it will either do nothing at all, or even exasperate the mischief. That it will do every thing is absurd; that it will do nothing is more so ; every statesman, that is, every true statesman, of every age and nation has considered a moral, steady, obedient, and united people, indispensable to external greatness or internal peace. Wise men have marked out the road whereby these desirable ends may be attained ; I will not multiply authorities; I will quote two only, the one secular, the other sacred.—" I think I may say," observes the famous John Locke, " that, of all the men we meet with, nine parts in ten are what they are, good or evil, useful or not, by their education. It is that which makes the great difference in mankind." " Train up a child," said Solomon, " in the way he should go; and when he is old he will not depart from it."

Now, has any man ever shewn by what other means we may arrive at this most necessary consummation ? If it be required in small states and even in despotic monarchies ; much more is it required in populous kingdoms and free governments;—and such is our position—our lot is cast in a time when our numbers, already vast, are hourly increasing at an almost geometric ratio—our institutions receive, every day, a more liberal complexion, while the democratic principle, by the mere force of circumstances, is fostered and developed—the public safety demands, each year, a larger measure of enlightenment and self-control; of enlightenment that all may understand their real interests ; of self-control that individual passion may be repressed to the advancement of public welfare. I know not where to search for these things but in the lessons and practice of the Gospel : true Christianity is essentially favourable to freedom of institutions in Church and State, because it imparts a judgment of your own and another's rights, a sense of public and private duty, an enlarged philanthropy and self-restraint, unknown to those democracies of former times, which are called, and only called, the polished nations of antiquity.

Sir, I do not deny, very far from it, the vast and meritorious efforts of the National Society; nor will I speak disparagingly of the efforts of some of the dissenting bodies; but in spite of all that has been done, a tremendous waste still remains uncultivated, "a great and terrible wilderness," that I shall now endeavour to lay open before you.

Sir, the population of England and Wales in the year 1801 was 8,872,980; in 1841 it had risen to 15,906,829, shewing an increase in less than half a century on the whole population of 7,033,849. If I here take one-fifth (which is understated, one-fourth being the ordinary calculation,) as the number supposed to be capable of some education, there will result a number of 3,181,365; deducting one third as provided for at private expense, there will be left a number of 2,120,910; deducting also for children in union workhouses, 50,000; and lastly deducting 10 per cent. for accidents and casualties, 212,091; there will then be the number of 1,858,819 to be provided for at the public expense. Now by the tables in the excellent pamphlet of the Rev. Mr. Burgess, of Chelsea, it appears that the total number of daily scholars, in connection with the Established church, is 749,626. By the same tables, the total number of daily scholars, in connection with dissenting bodies, is stated at 95,000; making a sum total of daily scholars in England and Wales, 844,626: leaving, without any daily instruction the number of 1,014,193 persons. These tables are calculated upon the returns of 1833, with an estimate for the increase of the Church of England scholars since those returns, and with an allowance in the same proportion for the increase of the dissenting scholars. But if we look forward to the next ten years, there will be an increase of at least 2,500,000 in the population; and should nothing be done to supply our want, we shall then have in addition to our present arrears, a fearful multitude of untutored savages.

Next, I find as a sample of the state of adult and juvenile delinquency, that the number of committals in the year 1841 was, of persons of all ages, 27,760; and of persons under the age of sixteen years, the proportion was 11½ per cent. I quote these tables in conformity with established usage and ancient prejudice; but they are, with a view to any accurate estimate of the moral condition of the kingdom, altogether fallacious—they do not explain to us whether the cases be those of distinct criminals, or in many instances, those of the same individuals reproduced: if the proportion be increased we have no clue to the discovery whether it be real or fictitious, permanent or casual; if diminished, we congratulate each other, but without examining how far the diminution must be ascribed to an increased morality, or a more effective Police—it is very well to rely on an effective Police for short and turbulent periods; it is ruinous to rely on it for the government of a generation.—For after all, how much there must ever be perilous to the state, and perilous to society, which, whether it be manifested or not, is far beyond the scope of magisterial power, and curable only by a widely different process! I will not, therefore, attempt a comparison of one period of crime with another; if the matters be worse, my case is established; if better, they can be so only through the greater diffusion of external morality. That morality, then, which is so effective even on the surface of the nation, it should be our earnest and constant endeavour to root deeply in their hearts.

Having stated this much in a general way, I will now take a few of those details which form a part of the complement of this mass of wickedness and mischief—we shall thus learn the principal seats of the danger, its character and extent locally, and in a great degree, the mode and nature of the remedy.

Sir, there have been laid upon the table within the last few days, a report by Mr. Horner and Mr. Saunders, inspectors of factories; and also the second report of the Childrens' Employment Commission; from these documents I shall draw very largely; and I wish to take this opportunity, as their final report has now been presented, of expressing to the commissioners, my sincere and heartfelt thanks for an exercise of talent and vigour, never before surpassed by any public servants.

The first town that I shall refer to is Manchester—some of those details I shall now quote I stated in the last session; but I shall venture to state them again as they bear immediately on the question before us. By the police returns of Manchester made up to December, 1841, we find the number of persons taken into custody during that year, was 13,345. Discharged by magistrates without punishment, 10,208; of these, under 20 years of age, there were males, 3,069; and females, 745. By the same returns to July 1842, (six months), there were taken into custody, 8,341; (This would make in a whole year, were the same proportion observed, 16,682;) of these, males 5,810; females 2,531. Now as to their instruction; with a knowledge of reading only, or reading and writing imperfectly, males, 1,999; females, 863. Neither read nor write, males, 3,098; females, 1,519;—total of these last 4,617. At 15 and under 20, 2,360; of these, males 1,639; females 721. But take what may be called the "curable" portion, and there will be, at 10 years and under 15, 665; males 547, females 118. Discharged by the magistrates in 182, without punishment (six months), 6,307, or at the rate of 12,614 in a year. Can the House be surprised at this statement, when the means for supplying opportunities to crime and the practice of debauchery are so abundant? It appears that there are in Manchester—Pawnbrokers, 129 ; this may be a symptom of distress ; beer houses 769 ; public houses 498 ; brothels 309; ditto, lately suppressed, 111; ditto, where prostitutes are kept, 163; ditto, where they resort, 223 ; street-walkers in borough, 763 ; thieves residing in the borough who do nothing but steal, 212 ; persons following some lawful occupation, but augmenting their gains by habitual violation of the law, 160; houses for receiving stolen goods, 63 ; ditto, suppressed lately, 32; houses for resort of thieves, 103; ditto, lately suppressed, 25 ; lodging-houses where sexes indiscriminately sleep together, 109.

But there is another cause that aids the progress of crime which prevails in the town of Manchester. I will mention the fact that a vast number of children of the tenderest years, either through absence or through neglect of their parents, I do not now say which, are suffered to roam at large through the streets of the town, contracting the most idle and profligate habits. I have here a return that I myself moved for in the year 1836, and I see that the number of children found wandering in the streets, and restored to their parents by the police in 1835, was no less than 8,650, in 1840 it was reduced to 5,500—having heard this table the House will not be surprised at the observations I am about to read from a gentleman of long and practical knowledge of the place. " What chance," says he, " have these children of becoming good members of society ? These unfortunates gradually acquire vagrant habits, become beggars, vagrants, criminals. It does not appear unfair to calculate that in the borough of Manchester 1,500 children are added to

' les classes dangereuses' annually. Besides," he adds, " the moral evil produced by these 1,500, let a calculation be made how much moneyper annum this criminal class costs the state."

I will next take the town of Birmingham; and it will be seen by the police returns for 1841, that the number of persons who were taken into custody was 5,556, of these the males were 4,537, and the females 1,018. Of these there could neither read nor write, 2,711 ; who could read only and write imperfectly, 2,504 ; read and write well, 206 ; having superior instruction, 36. I feel that it is necessary to apologise to the House for troubling them with such minute details; nevertheless, details such as these are absolutely indispensable. Now from a report on the state of education in the town of Birmingham, made by the Birmingham Statistical Society—one of those useful bodies which have sprung up of late years, and which give to the public a great mass of information, that may be turned to the best purposes—I find that the total number of schools of all kinds in the town of Birmingham is 669 ; but then the society calls everything a school where a child receives any sort of instruction, perhaps in a place more fitted to be a sty or coal-hole. Now out of the whole mass of the entire population of Birmingham there were 27,659 scholars. A vast proportion of these schools are what are called " dame schools;" and what these are in truth, may be known by the surveyors' report, who says of them, " moral and religious instruction forms no part of the system in dame-schools. A mistress in one of this class of schools on being asked whether she gave moral instruction to her scholars, replied ' No, I can't afford it at 3d a week.' Several did not know the meaning of the question. Very few appeared to think it was a part of their duty."—This, then, being the number of the schools for educating the young, and the character of the education imparted to them, I may now be allowed to state what are the means for the practice of vice. From the police returns for 1840, it appears that the number of these places is 998, and they are thus distributed:—Houses for reception of stolen goods, 81 ; ditto for resort of thieves, 228; brothels where prostitutes are kept, 200; houses of ill-fame, where they resort 110; number of houses where they lodge, 187 ; number of mendicants' lodging houses, 122; houses where sexes sleep indiscriminately together, 47—998; add to this, public-houses, 577 ; beer shops, 573. I will close this part by reading to the House an extract from a report, made by a committee of medical gentlemen in Birmingham, who, in the most benevolent spirit, devoted themselves to an examination of the state of Birmingham ; and who, looking to the removal of the growing evils that threaten the population, assert, that ' the first and most prominent suggestion is, the better education of the females in the arts of domestic economy. To the extreme ignorance of domestic management, on the part of the wives of the mechanics, is much of the misery and want of comfort to be traced. Numerous instances have occurred to us of the confirmed drunkard who attributes his habits of dissipation to a wretched home."

I will next take the town of Leeds ; and there it will be seen that the police details would be very similar in character, though differing in number, to those of Manchester and Birmingham—the report of the state of Leeds for 1838, is to this effect:—"It appears that the early periods of life furnish the greatest portion of criminals. Children of seven, eight, and nine years of age are not unfrequently brought before magistrates; a very large portion under 14 years. The parents are, it is to be feared in many instances, the direct causes of their crime."

" The spirit of lawless insubordination (says Mr. Symons
the sub-commissioner) which prevails at Leeds among the
children is very manifest: it is matter for painful appre-
hension." James Child, an inspector of police, states
that which is well worthy of the attention of the House :
He says there is " a great deal of drunkenness, especially
among the young people. I have seen children very little
higher than the table at these shops. There are some
beer-shops where there are rooms up stairs, and the boys
and girls, old people, and married of both sexes, go up
two by two, as they can agree, to have connection. . . . .
I am sure that sexual connection begins between boys and
girls at 14 and 15 years old." John Stubbs, of the police
force, confirms the above testimony. " We have," he says,
" a deal of girls on the town under 15, and boys who live
by thieving. There are half a dozen beer shops where
none but young ones go at all. They support these
houses."

I will now turn to Sheffield :—The Rev. Mr. Livesey,
the minister of St. Philip's, having a population of 24,000,
consisting almost exclusively of the labouring classes,
gives in evidence,—" Moral condition of children . . . .
in numerous instances most deplorable. . . . . On Sunday
afternoons it is impossible to pass along the highways, &c.
beyond the police boundaries, without encountering numerous groups of boys, from 12 years and upwards, gaming for
copper coin . . . . the boys are early initiated into habits
of drinking. But the most revolting feature of juvenile
depravity is early contamination from the association of
the sexes. The outskirts of the town are absolutely
polluted by this abomination ; nor is the veil of darkness
nor seclusion always sought by these degraded beings.
Too often they are to be met in small parties, who appear
to associate for the purpose of promiscuous intercourse,

their ages being apparently about fourteen or fifteen."
The Rev. Mr. Farish states, " There are beer houses attended by youths exclusively, for the men will not have
them in the same houses with themselves." Hugh Parker,
Esq. a justice of the peace, remarks, " A great proportion
of the working classes are ignorant and profligate . . . .
the morals of their children exceedingly depraved and
corrupt . . . . given, at a very early age, to petty theft,
swearing and lying; during minority to drunkenness, debauchery, idleness, profanation of the Sabbath; dog and
prize-fighting." Mr. Rayner, the superintendent of police,
deposes, that " Lads from twelve to fourteen years of age
constantly frequent beer-houses, and have, even at that
age, their girls with them, who often incite them to commit petty thefts . . . . vices of every description at a very
early age . . . . great number of vagrant children
prowling about the streets . . . these corrupt the working
children. . . . . The habits of the adults confirm the
children in their vices." George Messon, a police officer,
adds, " There are many beer-shops which are frequented
by boys only . . . . as early as thirteen years of age.
The girls are many of them loose in their conduct, and
accompany the boys. . . . . I remember the Chartist
attack on Sheffield last winter. I am certain that a great
number of young lads were among them—some as young
as fifteen : they generally act as men." All this was confirmed by Daniel Astwood, also a police officer; by Mr.
George Crossland, registrar and vestry clerk to the board
of guardians ; by Mr. Ashley, master of the Lancasterian
school; by Dr. Knight, and by Mr. Carr, a surgeon. Mr.
Abraham, the inventor of the magnetic guard, remarks,
" There is most vice and levity and mischief in the class
who are between sixteen and nineteen. You see more
lads between seventeen and nineteen with dogs at their

heels and other evidences of dissolute habits." Mr. James
Hall and others of the working people say, the "morals
of the children are tenfold worse than formerly . . . .
There are beer shops frequented by boys from nine to
fifteen years old, to play for money and liquor." Charlotte
Kirkman, a poor woman of the operative class, aged 60,
observes ; and I much wish here to draw the attention of
the House, because it is extremely desirable that they
should know in what light, the best and most decent of the
working people regard these things, " I think morals are
getting much worse, which I attribute in a great measure
to the beer-shops. . . . . There were no such girls in my
time as there are now. When I was four or five and
twenty, my mother would have knocked me down if I
had spoken improperly to her. . . . Many have children
at 15. I think bastardy almost as common now as a
woman being in the family-way by her husband. . . . .
Now it's nothing thought about." " The evidence (says the
sub-commissioner), with very few exceptions, attests a melancholy amount of immorality among the children of the
working classes in Sheffield, and especially among young
persons. Within a year of the time of my visit," he continues, " the town was preserved from an organised scheme
to fire and plunder it, merely by the information of one man,
and the consequent readiness of the troops. A large body of
men and boys marched on it in the dead of the night; and
a very large quantity of crowsfeet to lame horses, pikes,
and combustibles were found on them, at their houses,
and left on the road. Several were pledged to fire their
own houses. I name this, as a further illustration of the
perilous ignorance and vice prevailing among that young
class between boys and full grown men, who were known
to be among the chief actors in these scenes."

Mr. Symons—and I shall the more effectively quote his

opinions, because he is most strongly opposed to the political views which I venture to hold—further says, and it is right that I should state it in justice to so excellent a body of men : " If vice increases in Sheffield, the blame assuredly rests not on the clergy ; few towns are blessed with so pious or active a ministry.   It is not for want of exertion on their parts, if the churches and chapels are unfilled, and the schools scantily attended ; and this remark applies also to part of the Wesleyan and some other religious denominations."

I shall now proceed to another district, to Wolverhampton, and there I find Mr. Horne giving the following description :—" Among all the children and young persons I examined, I found, with very few exceptions, that their minds were as stunted as their bodies ; their moral feelings stagnant. . . . . The children and young persons possess but little sense of moral duty towards their parents, and have little affection for them. . . . . One child believed that Pontius Pilate and Goliath were apostles ; another, fourteen or fifteen years of age, did not know how many two and two made.   In my evidence taken in this town alone, as many as five children and young persons had never heard even the name of Jesus Christ. . . . . You will find boys who have never heard of such a place as London, and of Willenhall, (only three miles distant,) who have never heard of the name of the Queen, or of such names as Wellington, Nelson, Bonaparte, or King George." " But," (adds the commissioner) " while of scripture names I could not, in general, obtain any rational account, many of the most sacred names never having even been heard, there was a general knowledge of the lives of Dick Turpin and Jack Sheppard, not to mention the preposterous epidemic of a hybrid negro song."—This we may suppose is an elegant periphrasis for the popular song of " Jim Crow."—Mr.

Horne goes on to say—"The master of the British School deposes, 'I have resided, as a teacher, for the last six years, during which I have observed that the character and habits of the numerous labouring poor are of the lowest order.' The master of the National School says 'besotted to the last degree.'"—Sir, there are many things of an extremely horrid description to be detailed concerning the physical condition of the children in these parts, but I forbear to touch them at present, being engaged only on their moral deficiency.

I now go to Willenhall, and there it is said,—" A lower condition of morals cannot, I think, be found—they sink some degrees (when that is possible) below the worst classes of children and young persons in Wolverhampton ; they do not display the remotest sign of comprehension as to what is meant by the term of morals." Next, of Wednesfield, it is said the population are " much addicted to drinking ; many besotted in the extreme; poor dejected men, with hardly a rag to their backs, are often seen drunk two or three days in the week, and even when they have large families." The same profligacy and ignorance at Darlaston, where we have the evidence of three parties, an overseer, a collector, and a relieving officer, to a very curious fact; I quote this to shew the utter recklessness and intellectual apathy in which these people live, caring little but for existence and the immediate physical wants of the passing hour ; they state, " that there are as many as 1,00⁄ men in Darlaston who do not know their own names, only their nicknames." But it is said, that in Bilston things are much better. It is remarked that the "moral condition of children and young persons on the whole was very superior to that in Wolverhampton;" he excepts, however, "the bank-girls, and those who work at the screw-manufactories." Among them, "great numbers of bastards;" the bank-girls drive coal-carts, ride astride upon horses, drink, swear, fight, smoke, whistle, sing, and care for nobody." Here I must observe, if things are better in Bilston, it is owing to the dawn of education, " to the great exertions of the Rev. Mr. Fletcher, and the Rev. Mr. Owen, in the church ; and Mr. Robert Bew, (chemist,) and Mr. Dimmock, (iron merchant,) among the dissenters." Next, as to Sedgeley, " children and young persons," says the rector, "grow up in irreligion, immorality, and ignorance. The number of girls at nailing considerably exceeds that of the boys; it may be termed the district of female blacksmiths; constantly associating with depraved adults, and young persons of the opposite sex, they naturally fall into all their ways; and drink, smoke, swear, &c. &c. and become as bad as men. The men and boys are usually naked, except a pair of trowsers ; the women and girls have only a thin ragged petticoat, and an open shirt without sleeves."— Look to Warrington; the Honourable and Reverend Horace Powys, the rector, says, and there is no man more capable, from talent and character, of giving an opinion,— " My conviction is—and it is founded on the observation of some years—that the general condition of the children employed in labour in this town is alarmingly degraded, both religiously, morally, and intellectually." And here, too, is the evidence of the Rev. John Molyneux, a Roman Catholic priest, who began by stating his peculiar qualifications to give testimony, having a congregation of three thousand persons, and chiefly among the poorer classes. " Children in pin-works," he said, "are very immoral—they sit close together, and encourage each other in cursing and swearing, and loose conversation, which I grant you they do not understand,"—a conclusion in which I can not agree :—" but it renders them he adds prone to adopt the acts of immorality on which they converse."—;" Those girls

17

who from very early labour at pins go to the factories, do not ever make good housekeepers : they have no idea of it; neither of economy, nor cooking, nor mending their clothes."

Next, Sir, I will examine the Potteries. Mr. Scriven, the sub-commissioner, uses these expressions :—" I almost tremble, however, when I contemplate the fearful deficiency of knowledge existing throughout the district, and the consequences likely to result to this increased and increasing population. . . . . It will appear," he adds, " by the evidence from Cobridge and Burslem, that more than three-fourths of the persons therein named can neither read nor write. . . . . It is not from my own knowledge," he continues, " that I proclaim their utter, their absolute ignorance. I would respectfully refer you to the evidence of their own pastors and masters, and it will appear that, as one man, they acknowledge and lament their low and degraded condition." Mr. Lowndes, clerk to the board of guardians of the Burslem union, says : " It is with pain that I have witnessed the demoralizing effects of the system, as it has hitherto existed. . . . . It appears to me fraught with incalculable evils, both physical and moral." Mr. Grainger, a sub-commissioner, in his report respecting Nottingham, writes : " All parties, clergy, police, manufacturers, workpeople, and parents, agree that the present system is a most fertile source of immorality. . . . The natural results . . . . have contributed in no slight degree, to the immorality which, according to the opinion universally expressed, prevails to a most awful extent in Nottingham. Much of the existing evil is to be traced to the vicious habits of parents, many of whom are utterly indifferent to the moral and physical welfare of their offspring." " Education of the girls more neglected even than that of boys. . . . . Vast majority of females utterly ignorant. . . . . Impossible to overstate evils which result

c

from this deplorable ignorance." . . . . " The medical practitioners of Birmingham forcibly point out the ' misery which ensues; improvidence, absence of all comfort, neglect of children, and alienation of all affection in families, and drunkenness on the part of the husband.' " And here I have to call the attention of the House to the testimony of a most respectable person, a simple mechanic; and I am very anxious to put forward the views of this individual; because, his statements are the result of long and personal experience. I refer to the evidence of Joseph Corbett, a mechanic of Birmingham. I confess that I should like to read the whole of the report. I recom-mend it strongly to your attention; it will be found in the appendix to Mr. Grainger's report. I cannot, however, refrain from quoting one or two passages of it. " I have seen," he says, " the entire ruin of many families from the waste of money and bad conduct of fathers and sons seeking amusement and pastime in an alehouse. From no other single cause alone does half so much demor-alization and misery proceed." He then adds, "from my own experience," and here he spoke with feeling on the subject, for he referred to what he had seen in his own home, and what he had witnessed with respect to his parents :—" My own experience tells me that the instruc-tion of the females in the work of a house, in teaching them to produce cheerfulness and comfort at the fireside, would prevent a great amount of misery and crime. There would be fewer drunken husbands and disobedient chil-dren. . . . . As a working man, within my observation, female education is disgracefully neglected. I attach more importance to it than to anything else." I cannot think that any one will be displeased to hear such sentiments coming from a man in the situation of Joseph Corbett. Take this as a proof of what the working people may be brought to, if they cease to be so utterly neglected. This is an instance, among many, to shew what thousands of right-hearted Englishmen, if you would but train them, you might raise up among the ranks of the operative classes.

This, Sir, is pretty nearly the whole of the statements which I have to make as to these districts; but there are other opinions, by persons of great authority on this subject, and which, with the permission of the House, I will read, although I have not permission to give the names of the writers. One gentleman, whose opportunities of observation are unequalled, speaks of " the present existence of a highly demoralised middle-aged and rising generation, worse and more debased than, I believe, any previous generation for the last three hundred years." A clergyman, writing from one of the disturbed districts, says :—" The moral condition of the people is as bad as it is possible to be. Vice is unrebuked, unabashed; moral character of no avail. * * * A spirit of disaffection prevails almost universally — magistrates, masters, pastors, and all superiors, are regarded as enemies and oppressors." Another, in writing from the disturbed districts, states :—" I took down myself the following words, as they fell from the lips of a Chartist orator—' The prevalence of intemperance and other vicious habits was the fault of the aristocracy and the mill-owners, who had neglected to provide the people with sufficient means of moral improvement, and would form an item of that great account which they would one day be called upon to render to a people indignant at the discovery of their own debasement.' Another remarked:— ' A working man's hall is opened on Sundays; and in this, 300 poor children are initiated into infidel and seditious principles.' Another said :—' A wild and satanic spirit is infused into the hearers.' " An officer of great experience to whom I put the question—" What are the consequences to be apprehended if the present state of things be suffered to continue ?" replies—' Unless a speedy alteration be made in the manufacturing districts, a fresh and more extensive outbreak will again occur, threatening loss to the whole nation.' "

Sir, I must now remark, that this condition of things prevails, more or less, throughout the whole of England, but particularly in the manufacturing and trading districts. The evil is not partial, it is almost universally diffused over the surface of the country. The time I might be allowed to occupy would be insufficient for me to travel through the whole of the details; but the House will find, in the second report of the Children's Employment Commission, which is devoted to the statement of their moral condition, the proof that it everywhere afflicts the country—it is nearly universal throughout the whole of the coal and iron-fields of Great Britain and Wales.— Look to the east of Scotland—one clergyman says :— " The condition of the lower classes is daily becoming worse in regard to education ; and it is telling every day upon the moral and economic condition of the adult population." Another clergyman remarks : —" The country will be inevitably ruined, unless some steps are taken by the Legislature to secure education to the children of the working classes." Of North Wales we see it stated :— " Not one collier-boy in ten can read, so as to comprehend what he reads :" while of South Wales it is observed :—" Many are almost in a state of barbarism. Religious and moral training is out of the question. I should certainly be within bounds by saying that not one grown male or female in fifty can read." In the West of Scotland I find the same class of persons described as follows:—" A large portion of the colliery and ironwork hands are living in an utterly depraved state, a moral degradation, which is entailing misery and disease on themselves, and disorder on the community." There is an equally lamentable state of things existing in Yorkshire, Durham, Lancashire, North Staffordshire and Cumberland. The replies of many of the children who were questioned by the commissioners, shewe a state of things utterly disgraceful to the character of a Christian country. One of the children replied to a question put to him: " I never heard of France; I never heard of Scotland or Ireland; I do not know what America is." James Taylor, a boy eleven years old, said that he " has never heard of Jesus Christ; has never heard of God, but has heard the men in the pit say ' God damn them;' never heard of London." A girl eighteen years old, said, " I never heard of Christ at all." This indeed, the commissioner adds, is very common among children and young persons. She proceeded to say, " I never go to church or chapel;" again, " I don't know who God is." The sub-commissioner who visited Halifax, has recorded this sentence: " You have expressed surprise, says an employer, at Thomas Mitchell not having heard of God; I judge there are very few colliers here about that have."

Now can it be possible that such a state of things should exist without being attended with the most pernicious consequences? but, I will go further, and rejoice that it is not possible — an evil unfelt is an evil unseen; nothing but an urgent and a biting necessity will rouse us to action from our fancied security.

First, Sir, observe the effects that are produced by the drunken habits of the working-classes; you cannot have a more unanswerable proof of the moral degradation of a people. I know it is frequently asserted that inebriety has yielded, in many instances, to greater habits of tem-

perance; but suppose it to be so ; the abatement is merely
fractional ; and no guarantee is given, in an improved morality, that those persons will not return to their former vicious courses—the abatement, however, has not taken place,
at least in those districts which were lately subjected to the
enquiries of the Commissioners. Will the House now listen to some statements on this subject, which, lamentable
as is the condition they disclose, describe but a tenth part
of the evils springing out of this sad propensity? In the
year 1834 a Committee was appointed on the motion of
Mr. Buckingham, to investigate the causes and effects of
drunkenness. That Committee produced a report, which,
by the by, has never received a tithe of the attention so
valuable a document deserved ; from that report we learn
that the sum annually expended by the working-people in
the consumption of ardent spirits is estimated at twenty-
five millions! and " I have no doubt," says a witness of
great experience, " that it is, in fact, to a much larger extent." ˙ I wrote to the chaplain of a county jail, a gentleman of considerable observation and judgment, and put to
him the following question,—" How much of the crime
that brings prisoners to the jail can you trace to habits of
intoxication?" Now mark his reply; "In order to arrive
at a just conclusion, I devoted several nights to a careful
examination of the entries in my journals for a series of
years, and although I had been impressed previously with
a very strong conviction, derived from my own personal experience in attendance on the sick poor, that the practice
of drinking was the great moral pestilence of the kingdom,
I was certainly not prepared for the frightful extent to
which I find it chargeable with the production of crime : I
am within the mark in saying that three-fourths of the
crime committed is the result of intemperance." In corro-
boration of this, I will appeal to the very valuable evidence

given by Mr. J. Smith, the governor of the prison in Edinburgh. That witness states—"Having been for a number of years a missionary among the poor in Edinburgh, and having for two years had the charge of the house of refuge for the destitute, I have had, perhaps, the best opportunities of observing how far drunkenness produced ignorance, destitution, and crime; and the result of my experience is a firm conviction that, but for the effects of intemperance, directly and indirectly, instead of having five hundred prisoners in this prison at this time, there would not have been fifty."

The next document to which I shall refer, I regard as of a most important nature, and as one which deserves the most serious attention of the House. It is a memorial drawn up by a body of working men at Paisley, and addressed to their employers. It bears assuredly a remarkable testimony as to the moral effects of intemperance. I entertain a strong opinion of the great value of this paper, not only from the opinions which it expresses, but because it developes the sentiments of that class who are the agents and victims of this disastrous habit, and who speak, therefore, from practical knowledge. It states that " drunkenness is most injurious to the interests of the weavers as a body: drunkards are always on the brink of destitution. There can be no doubt that whatever depresses the moral worth of any body of workmen, likewise depresses their wages; and whatever elevates that worth, enables them to obtain and procure higher wages." This, Sir, in my opinion, is as sound political economy as ever has been spoken, written, or published. Again, I find it stated in the report of Mr. Buckingham's committee, that the estimated value of the property lost or deteriorated by drunkenness, either by shipwreck or mischiefs of a similar character, was not less than £50,000,000 a year.—These are the financial losses ; and it may be easy to estimate, with sufficient accuracy, the pecuniary damage that society undergoes by these pernicious practices ; but it is not so easy to estimate the moral and social waste, the intellectual suffering and degradation which follow in their train. To that end I must here invite the attention of the House to evidence of another description ; I will lay before them the testimony of eminent medical men, who will shew what ruin of the intellect and the disposition attends the indulgence of these vicious enjoyments—we shall see how large a proportion of the cases of lunacy is ascribable to intoxication ; but we shall draw, moreover, this startling conclusion, that, if thousands from this cause are deprived of their reason and incarcerated in mad-houses, there must be many-fold more who, though they fall short of the point of absolute insanity, are impaired in their understanding and moral perceptions. The first medical authority to which I shall refer, is a very eminent physician, well known to many members of this house, I mean Dr. Corsellis, of the Wakefield Lunatic Asylum : " I am led," he says, " to believe that intemperance is the exciting cause of insanity in about one-third of the cases of this institution ;" and he adds, " the proportion at Glasgow is about twenty-six per cent., and at Aberdeen eighteen per cent." Dr. Browne, of the Crichton Asylum, Dumfries, says—" The applications for the introduction of individuals who have lost reason from excessive drinking continue to be very numerous." At Northampton, the superintendent of the asylum says —" Amongst the causes of insanity intemperance predominates." At Montrose, Dr. Poole, the head of the asylum, says—" Twenty-four per cent. of insane cases from intemperance." Dr. Prichard, who is well known, not only in the medical, but also in the literary world, writes to me that—" The medical writers of all countries reckon intemperance among the most influential exciting causes of insanity. Esquirol, who has been most celebrated on the continent for his researches into the statistics of madness, and who is well known to have extended his enquiries into all countries, was of opinion that " this cause gives rise to one-half of the cases of insanity that occur in Great Britain." Dr. Prichard adds that " this fact, although startling, is confirmed by many instances. It was found that, in an asylum at Liverpool, to which four hundred and ninety-five patients had been admitted, not less than two hundred and fifty-seven had become insane from intemperance." It is confirmed as a scientific fact by statements of American physicians almost without exception. Dr. Rensselaer, of the United States, says, that, " in his opinion, one half of the cases of insanity which came under the care of medical men in that country arose more or less from the use of strong drink."—These things, Sir, not only inflict misery and suffeirng on a very large class of the present community, but they entail a heavy loss on the country at large. It cannot be denied that the state has an interest in the health and strength of her sons ; but the effects of various diseases on one generation are transmitted with intensity to another! I may also mention, to support these opinions, that the number of admissions to the Somerset Hospital, Cape Town, in the course of a year and nine months, was 1,050, and of these not less than 763 were the result of intemperance. It was also found, by *post mortem* examinations, that in the same period the number of deaths in that hospital, which was caused by intemperance, was not less than eight out of ten. Now look to the pauperism it produces ; one instance shall suffice : Mr. Chadwick gave in evidence before the Committee on Drunkenness, in 1834,—"The contractor for the management of the poor in Lambeth, and other parishes, stated to me that he once investigated the cause of pauperism in the cases of paupers then under his charge. The inquiry, he says, was conducted for some months, as I investigated every new case, and I found in nine cases out of ten the main cause was the ungovernable inclination for fermented liquors."

Next, Sir, vice is expensive to the public ; Mr. Collins, in his valuable statistics of Glasgow, observes,—" The people will cost us much, whether we will or not ; if we will not suffer ourselves to be taxed for their religious instruction, we must suffer to be taxed for the punishment and repression of crime." I will now just give a short estimate of the amount of the expense to which the country is subjected directly for the suppression of crime. I find that the expense of jails in 1841 was £137,449 ; during the same period the expense of houses of correction was £129,163 ; making together a total of £256,612. The expense of criminal prosecutions in 1841 was £170,521 ; the charge for the conveyance of prisoners was £23,242 ; the charge for the conveyance of transports to the hulks, &c. £8,195 ; and the expense for vagrants £7,167. These items make together the sum of £209,125. The expense of the rural police, and it should be remembered that this is only for a few counties, is £139,228. Thus the charges under the three heads which I have mentioned, amount, in a single year, to £604,965. But here, Sir, is a document well deserving, I think, of the attention of the House,—a curious illustration of the facts we are asserting; I have not been able to verify it myself, but I will take it as stated—In the county of Lancaster, in 1832, the number of criminal cases tried at the assizes was 126, and the average charge for each of them £40. The number of cases tried at the sessions was 2,587, and the average charge for each of these was £7. 19s. The aggregate amount of charge was £25,656. Now in addition to this average charge, let us take the estimate cost for the transportation across the seas of each person convicted at £25. This would be a gross sum for the cost of each prosecution of £65;—if the calculation, then, of Mr. Burgess be correct, that eleven shillings in the year will supply the education of one child for that term, we must confess that for the expense of a single convict, we might, during the space of twelve months, give moral and religious education to one hundred and seventeen children. Nevertheless, Sir, it is a melancholy fact, that while the country disburses the sums I have mentioned, and more too, for the punishment of crime, the State devotes but thirty thousand a year to the infusion of virtue ; and yet, I ask you, could you institute a happier and healthier economy in your finances, than to reduce your criminal, so to speak, and increase your moral expenditure ? Difficulties may lie in your way; mortifications may follow your attempts, but you cannot fail of raising some to the dignity of virtuous men, and many to the rank of tranquil and governable citizens.

I have not here included an estimate of the loss inflicted on society by plunder, violence, and neglect; nor can I arrive at it; it must, however, be necessarily very large. Let us use as an approximation, a statement made by a late member of this House (Mr. Slaney) that, in one year, in the town of Liverpool alone, the loss by plunder was calculated at the enormous sum of seven hundred thousand pounds.

Thus far, Sir, I have endeavoured to lay before you an outline of our present condition, and to collect, into one point of view, a few of the more prominent mischiefs. A partial remedy for these evils will be found in the moral and religious culture of the infant mind ; but this is not all : we must look further, and do more, if we desire to place the working-classes in such a condition that, the lessons they have learned as children, they may have freedom to practise as adults.

Now, if it be true, as most undoubtedly it is, that the
State has a deep interest in the moral and physical prosperity of all her children, she must not terminate her care
with the years of infancy, but extend her control and providence over many other circumstances that affect the
working-man's life. Without entering here into the nature
and variety of those practical details, which might be ad-
vantageously taught in addition to the first and indispensable elements, we shall readily perceive that many
things are requisite, even to the adult, to secure to him, so
far as is possible, the well-being of his moral and physical
condition. I speak not now of laws and regulations to
abridge, but to enlarge his freedom; not to limit his
rights, but to multiply his opportunities of enjoying them;
laws and regulations which shall give him what all confess
to be his due; which shall relieve him from the danger of
temptations he would willingly avoid, and under which he
cannot but fall; and which shall place him, in many as-
pects of health, happiness, and possibilities of virtue, in that
position of independence and security, from which, under
the present state of things, he is too often excluded.

Sir, there are many evils of this description which might
be urged; but I shall name three only, as indications of
what I mean, and as having a most injurious and
most lasting effect on the moral and physical condition
of an immense portion of our people. I will briefly state
them; and there will then be no difficulty in shewing their
connection with the present motion; and how deep and
how immediate is their influence on the morals of infants
and adults, of children and parents; and how utterly
hopeless are all systems of education, so long as you suffer
them extensively to prevail.

The first I shall take is the truck system. Now hear
what Mr. Horne, the sub-commissioner, says on this subject:—"The truck system encourages improvidence, by

preventing the chance of a habit of saving, for nobody can save food. It prevents a family from obtaining a sufficient supply of clothes, and more comfortable furniture, in proportion to the possession of which it is always found that the working-man becomes more steady, industrious, and careful. It therefore amounts to a prevention of good conduct." In another place, he says: "The poor working man never sees the colour of a coin, all his wages are consumed in food, and of the very worst quality; and to prevent the chance of his having a single penny in his possession, the reckonings were postponed from week to week, until sometimes two or three months had elapsed." Now, as to the corrupting effects of this system, Mr. Horne, in his report, emphatically says:— "One final remark should, however, be made on the particular evil of the system, which principally relates to the moral condition of the children and young persons, nothing can be worse than the example set by the truck system—an example which is constantly before the eyes of the children, and in which they grow up, familiarised with the grossest frauds, the subtlest tricks, and the most dishonest evasions, habitually practised by their masters, parents, and other adults, in the very face of law and justice, and with perfect impunity." Such is the result of this part of the inquiry made by Mr. Horne. That gentleman uses the emphatic language that the truck system not only familiarises the mind, and the mind too of the child, with the grossest frauds, but that it tends to prevent the practice of any of the moral virtues. See, too, the effect as stated in the evidence produced before Parliament. It is notorious that the system has led to the most serious effects in several parts of the country. The whole man suffers; his experience; his thrifty habits; his resolutions of forethought; he is widely and justly discontented, becomes a bad subject, and ripe for mischief. In 1834 the existence of the truck system drove the mining districts of South Wales into open rebellion ; it produced the disturbances that took place in Staffordshire in 1842 ; and no one can calculate the flood of the moral and physical mischiefs that devastated those counties as the result of their outbreak.'

I will take, in the second place, the payment of wages in public-houses, beer-shops, and localities of that description. You have recognised the principle of interdicting such a practice in the Colliery-bill of last year ; let me shew how necessary it is that a law of that kind should become universal :—"Payments of wages in cash," says Mr. Horne, " are made in a public-house (for the convenience, they pretend, of change), where it is required that every man shall spend a shilling as a rule, which is to be spent in drink. Boys have also to spend proportionately to their wages (generally sixpence), and either they thus learn to drink by taking their share, or, if they cannot, some adult drinks it for them till they can. The keeper of this house generally delays the settling of accounts, so as to give more time for drinking previously." Now, Sir, I have frequently heard discredit thrown on the exertions that have been made to promote the improvement in the moral condition of the working classes, in consequence of the criminal conduct of some who had received a moral and religious education. No doubt it is true that persons may be found in jails who have received their education in Sunday and other schools ; but there is many a man who will trace his ruin to the practice I mention; whole families have been pauperized ; and, by a perverted logic, moral teaching itself is declared to be useless, because the system we allow has made moral practice next to impossible.

The third, is the state of the dwellings of the poor—I

will at once put before the House a picture drawn by an able hand ;—Captain Miller, the valuable superintendent of the police at Glasgow, writes thus : " In the very centre of the city there is an accumulated mass of squalid wretchedness, which is probably unequalled in any other town in the British dominions. There is concentrated every thing that is wretched, dissolute, loathsome, and pestilential. These places are filled by a population of many thousands of miserable creatures. The houses in which they live are unfit even for stys ; and every apartment is filled with a promiscuous crowd of men, women, and children : all in the most revolting state of filth and squalor. In many of the houses there is scarcely any ventilation ; dunghills lie in the vicinity of the dwellings; and from the extremely defective sewerages, filth of every kind constantly accumulates. In these horrid dens the most abandoned characters of the city are collected ; from whence they nightly issue to disseminate diseases, and to pour upon the town every species of crime and abomination."—Will any man after this tell me that it is to any purpose to take children for the purposes of education during two hours a day, and then turn them back for twenty-two to such scenes of vice, and filth, and misery ? I am quite certain this statement is not exaggerated, I have been on the spot and seen it myself; and not only there, but I have found a similar state of things existing at Leeds, at Manchester, and in London. It is impossible for language to describe the horrid and disgraceful scenes that are exposed to the sight in these places, and I am sure no one can recollect, without the most painful feelings, the thousands and hundreds of thousands, who ought to be the subjects of any system of education, that are hopelessly congregated in these dens of filth, of suffering, and infamy.

Turn, then, to the invaluable report of Mr. Chadwick on

the sanitary state of the population, which has just been presented to the House. He shews clearly how indispensable it is to establish some better regulations with regard to the residences of the people, if you wish to make them a moral and religious race, and that all your attempts at their reformation will be useless, if steps are not taken to promote their decency and comfort. He says, amongst the conclusions at which he arrives towards the end of his report:—" That the formation of all habits of cleanliness is obstructed by defective supplies of water; that the annual loss of life from filth and bad ventilation is greater than the loss from death or wounds in any wars in which the country has been engaged in modern times; that of the 43,000 cases of widowhood, and 112,000 cases of destitute orphanage, relieved from the poor's-rate in England alone, it appears that the greatest proportions of deaths of the heads of families occurred from the above specified and other removable causes ; that their ages were under forty-five years—that is to say, thirteen years below the natural probabilities of life, as shewn by the experience of the whole population of Sweden; that the younger population, bred up under noxious physical agencies, is inferior in physical organization and general health to a population preserved from the presence of such agencies; that the population, so exposed, is less susceptible of moral influences, and the effects of education are more transient, than with a healthy population ; that these adverse circumstances tend to produce an adult popu-lation short-lived, improvident, reckless, and intemperate, and with habitual avidity for sensual gratification ; that these habits lead to the abandonment of all the conveniences and the decencies of life, and especially lead to the over-crowding of their homes, which is destructive to the morality as well as to the health of large classes of both sexes ; that defective town-cleansing fosters habits of the most abject degradation, tending to the demoralization of large numbers of human beings, who subsist by means of what they find amid the various filth accumulated in neglected streets and by-places." Now, Sir, can any one gainsay the assertion that this state of things is cruel, disgusting, perilous?—indifference, despair, neglect of every kind—of the household, the children, the moral and the physical part—must follow in the train of such evils; the contemplation of them distresses the standers by, it exasperates the sufferer and his whole class, it breeds discontent and every bad passion; and then, when disaffection stalks abroad, we are alarmed, and cry out that we are fallen upon evil times, and so we are; but it is not because poverty is always seditious, but because wealth is too frequently oppressive.

This, Sir, completes the picture I desired to lay before the House: it has been imperfectly, and I fear tediously drawn. There is, however, less risk in taxing the patience than in taxing the faith of indulgent hearers. I have not presumed to propose a scheme, because I have ever thought that such a mighty undertaking demands the collective deliberation and wisdom of the executive, backed by the authority and influence of the Crown. But what does this picture exhibit. Mark, Sir, first, the utter inefficiency of our penal code—of our capital and secondary punishments. The country is wearied with pamphlets and speeches on gaol-discipline, model-prisons, and corrective processes; meanwhile crime advances at a rapid pace; many are discharged because they cannot be punished, and many become worse by the very punishment they undergo—punishment is disarmed of a large part of its terrors, because it no longer can appeal to any sense of shame;—and all this, because we will obstinately persist in setting our own wilfulness against the experience

D

of mankind and the wisdom of revelation, and believe that
we can regenerate the hardened man while we utterly
neglect his pliant childhood. You are right to punish
those awful miscreants who make a trade of blasphemy,
and pollute the very atmosphere by their foul exhibitions;
but you will never subdue their disciples and admirers,
except by the implements of another armoury. You must
draw from the great depository of truth all that can create
and refine a sound public opinion—all that can institute
and diffuse among the people the feelings and practices of
morality. I hope I am not dictatorial in repeating here,
that criminal tables and criminal statistics furnish no estimate of a nation's disorder. Culprits, such as they exhibit,
are but the representatives of the mischief, spawned by the
filth and corruption of the times. Were the crimes of
these offenders the sum total of the crimes of England,
although we should lament for the individuals, we might
disregard the consequences; but the danger is wider,
deeper, fiercer; and no one who has heard these statements and believes them, can hope that twenty years
more will pass without some mighty convulsion, and dis-
placement of the whole system of society.

Next, Sir, observe that our very multitude oppresses
us; and oppresses us, too, with all the fearful weight of a
blessing converted into a curse. The King's strength
ought to be in the multitude of his people; and so it is;
not, however, such a people as we must shortly have; but
in a people happy, healthy, and virtuous; "Sacra Deûm,
sanctique patres." Is that our condition of present com·
fort or prospective safety? You have seen in how many
instances the intellect is impaired, and even destroyed by
the opinions and practices of our moral world; honest
industry will decline, energy will be blunted, and whatever shall remain of zeal be perverted to the worst and

most perilous uses. An evil state of morals engenders
and diffuses a ferocious spirit; the mind of man is as
much affected by moral epidemics, as his body by disorders; thence arise murders, blasphemies, seditions,
every thing that can tear prosperity from nations, and
peace from individuals. See, Sir, the ferocity of disposition that your records disclose; look at the savage
treatment of children and apprentices; and imagine the
awful results, if such a spirit were let loose upon society.
Is the character of your females nothing?—and yet hear
the language of an eye-witness, and one long and deeply
conversant with their character; " They are becoming
similar to the female followers of an army, wearing the
garb of women, but actuated by the worst passions of
men; in every riot or outbreak in the manufacturing
districts the women are the leaders and exciters of the
young men to violence. The language they indulge
in is of the most horrid description—in short, while
they are demoralised themselves, they demoralise all
that come within their reach." People, Mr. Speaker,
will oftentimes administer consolation by urging that
a mob of Englishmen will never be disgraced by the
atrocities of the Continent. Now, Sir, apart from
the fact that one hundredth part of "the reign of
terror" is sufficient to annihilate all virtue and all peace
in society, we have never, except in 1780, and a few
years ago at Bristol and Nottingham, seen a mob of
our countrymen in triumphant possession. Conflagra-
tion then and plunder devastated the scene; nor were
they forgotten in the riots of last year, when, during the
short-lived anarchy of an hour, they fired I know not how
many houses within the district of the Potteries.

Consider, too, the rapid progress of time. In ten years
from this hour—no long period in the history of a nation—

all who are nine years of age will have reached the age of nineteen years; a period in which, with the few years that follow, there is the least sense of responsibility, the power of the liveliest action, and the greatest disregard of human suffering and human life. The early ages are of incalculable value; an idle reprobate of fourteen is almost irreclaimable; every year of delay abstracts from us thousands of useful fellow-citizens; nay, rather, it adds them to the ranks of viciousness, of misery, and of disorder. So long, Sir, as this plague-spot is festering among our people, all our labours will be in vain; our recent triumphs will avail us nothing—to no purpose, while we are rotten at heart, shall we toil to improve our finances, to expand our commerce, and explore the hidden sources of our difficulty and alarm. We feel that all is wrong, we grope at noonday as though it were night; disregarding the lessons of history and the Word of God, that there is neither hope nor strength, nor comfort, nor peace, but in a virtuous, a " wise, and an understanding people."

But, if we will retrace our steps, and do the first works—if we will apply ourselves earnestly, in faith and fear, to this necessary service, there lie before us many paths of peace, many prospects of encouragement. Turn where you will; examine the agents of every honest calling, and you will find that the educated man is the safest and the best in every profession. I might quote the testimony of distinguished officers, both military and naval, and they will tell you that no discipline is so vigorous as morality. I have here the earnest declaration of various manufacturers, that trustworthiness and skill will ever follow on religious training. You have heard the opinions of the judges at the late special assizes, more particularly the charge of that eminent lawyer and good man, Chief Justice Tindal. I have read correspondence of the clergy in the disturbed districts, and they boldly assert, that very few belonging to their congregations, and none belonging to their schools, were found among the insurgents against the public peace; because such persons well know that, however grievous their wrongs, they owe obedience to the laws, not on a calculation of forces, but for conscience' sake.

Nor let us, Sir, put out of mind this great and stirring consideration, that the moral condition of England seems destined by Providence to lead the moral condition of the world. Year after year we are sending forth thousands and hundreds of thousands of our citizens to people the vast solitudes and islands of another hemisphere; the Anglo-Saxon race will shortly overspead half the habitable globe. What a mighty and what a rapid addition to the happiness of mankind, if these thousands should carry with them, and plant in those distant regions, our freedom, our laws, our morality, and our religion!

This, Sir, is the ground of my appeal to this House; the plan that I venture to propose, and the argument by which I sustain it. It is, I know, but a portion of what the country requires; and even here we shall have, no doubt, disappointments to undergo, and failures to deplore; it will, nevertheless, bear for us abundant fruit. We owe to the poor of our land a weighty debt. We call them improvident and immoral, and so many of them are; but that improvidence and that immorality are the results, in a great measure, of our neglect, and, in not a little, of our example. We owe them, too, the debt of kinder language, and more frequent intercourse.—This is no fanciful obligation; our people are more alive than any other to honest zeal for their cause, and sympathy with their necessities, which, fall though it often-times may on unimpressible hearts, never fails to find some that it comforts, and many that it softens. Only let us declare, this night, that we will enter on a novel and a better course—that we will seek their temporal, through their eternal welfare—and the half of our work will then have been achieved. There are many hearts to be won, many minds to be instructed, and many souls to be saved : " *Oh Patria ! oh Divúm domus !*" —the blessing of God will rest upon our endeavours ; and the oldest among us may perhaps live to enjoy, for himself and for his children, the opening day of the immortal, because the moral glories of the British empire.

The following TABLE, showing the state of parts of London, which it was intended to quote, was accidentally omitted.

The London City Mission Report of two districts just examined, 1842 :—

In a small district immediately contiguous to Holborn Hill, found, families - - - - - -	103
Consisting of, persons - - - - -	391
From six years and upwards, could not read -	280
Of these, above twenty years of age - - -	119
In five courts and alleys in the Cow-cross district :—	
Heads of families - - - - - -	158
Cannot read - - - - - - -	102
Young persons, between seven and twenty-two -	106
Cannot read - - - - - - -	77

" Can we be surprised," says the Report, " at the number of public criminals ? Neighbourhoods such as these chiefly supply our jails with inmates. So late as October last there were in the House of Correction alone, 973 prisoners, exclusive of children, and out of these 717 had no education at all.''

JOHN OLLIVIER, PRINTER, 59, PALL MALL.

NEW PAMPHLETS.

A LETTER TO A LAYMAN,

ON THE RECENT CHANGES IN THE MANNER OF PERFORMING
DIVINE SERVICE IN THE METROPOLITAN CHURCHES.

By the Rev. T. TUNSTALL HAVERFIELD, M. A. 12mo. price 6d.

THREE SERMONS

ON THE SERVICE FOR THE ADMINISTRATION OF THE HOLY COMMUNION,

Preached on the 2nd, 3rd, and 4th Sundays in Advent, 1842, at St. James's Chapel,
York Street, by the Rev. T. TUNSTALL HAVERFIELD. Printed at the request of
the Congregation. 12mo. price 1s.

A SERMON ON THE NEGLECT AND APATHY

OF THE

PUBLIC IN THE PSALMODY AND RESPONSES IN THE CHURCH SERVICES.

By the Rev. W. J. E. BENNETT, M.A., Minister of Portman Chapel, Baker
Street, and late Student of Christ Church, Oxford.

THIRD EDITION. Price 6d.

FREE TRADE AND ITS CONSEQUENCES.

" Free Trade is a beautiful vision."—HENRY CLAY.

By W. WILLCOCKS SLEIGH, M.D.

Second edition, 8vo. price 6d.

Just published, price 2s. demy 8vo. pp. 104,

CHARACTER, MOTIVES, AND PROCEEDINGS

OF THE

ANTI-CORN LAW LEAGUERS,

WITH

A FEW GENERAL REMARKS ON THE CONSEQUENCES THAT
WOULD RESULT FROM A FREE TRADE IN CORN.

DEDICATED TO W. R. GREG, ESQ.

BY JOHN ALMACK, JUN.

PROFESSIONAL TRAINING AS AN ELEMENT OF SUCCESS
AND CONSERVATIVE INFLUENCE.

A

LECTURE

BEFORE THE

MEMBERS OF THE HARVARD LAW SCHOOL,

AT THE CLOSE OF THE TERM, JANUARY 11, 1861.

By EMORY WASHBURN, LL. D.,

UNIVERSITY PROFESSOR OF LAW.

BOSTON:
PUBLISHED BY THE HARVARD LAW SCHOOL.
1861.

Hon. EMORY WASHBURN,—

Dear Sir:—At a meeting of the School, this day held, it was unanimously voted to present to you the thanks of the School for the lecture with which you to-day closed the exercises of the term. We wish to assure you that your parting words shall not be unheeded, and that, however far we may go from the scene of common labor here, we never can forget the wisdom and kindness which have always marked all your relations to us, and of which the lecture this day is only one example.

Unwilling to trust its teachings to memory alone, the School has instructed us to ask of you a copy for publication. In the name of the School we now make that request.

We are, dear Sir, with great respect, your obedient servants,

MICHAEL W. ROBINSON,
EDWIN H. ABBOT,
HENRY A. WHITE,
Committee.

WRIGHT & POTTER, Printers, 4 Spring Lane, Boston.

Messrs. MICHAEL W. ROBINSON, EDWIN II. ABBOT, and HENRY A. WHITE,—

Gentlemen:—In complying with the flattering request which you have so kindly and courteously communicated to me, I have yielded my own preferences and judgment to the expressed wishes of others.

The lecture, the manuscript of which I herewith place in your hands, was never intended for the eye or ear of any one but the members of the Law School, to whom it was immediately addressed.

It was rather the impulse of feeling than the result of much reflection that led me to go beyond the limits of the few parting words of counsel and encouragement which the close of the term and the departure of many of the members of the School seemed to call for, and to remind them of the solemn duties and responsibilities which they were about to assume as citizens and as members of the profession which they had chosen, especially at this eventful crisis.

It seemed to me to be a fitting occasion to impress upon their minds what I regard as a solemn truth, that it requires only the same spirit of courtesy and forbearance, the same appreciation of, and respect for the rights and opinions of those who stand opposed to each other as citizens, which advocates, trained in the discipline of our profession, extend to one another in the controversies in which they are called to engage, to correct this acrimony of feeling and harshness of language which render local and sectional differences, in our country, so irritating and alarming.

I was especially encouraged to attempt this by the condition of the School itself. I found upon its catalogue, for the present year, the names of two hundred and fifty-two young men, gathered here from twenty-nine of the States of the Union. You yourselves represent localities as remote as Missouri, Massachusetts, and California. I found that of these, sixty-six had their homes in thirteen of the States, the District of Columbia included, in which that system is a recognized domestic institution which has been so fruitful an element of alienation between the different sections of our country. And yet, amidst the excitement which has been agitating the public mind outside of these walls, every thing within them has been characterized by calm and dispassionate harmony and good will.

It was not because these young men were not familiar with the causes of this agitation, nor was it that they did not share deeply in the feeling which prevailed in the several sections of the country with which they were connected. It was, in the first place, because they were so situated here that they could not fail to perceive that there were two sides to the question in controversy, and were able to apply other tests to its merits than that of mere feeling.

In the next place, their training, here and elsewhere, as gentlemen, taught them to regard the opinions of others, and this was aided by that habit of investigation which they had been cultivating as a part of the mental discipline of the School. Add to this, there were numerous ties of common sympathy which had naturally grown up between them, such ties as, but for the mischievous interference of rash and wicked men, might still bind our whole country together, under the influence of which, and the other causes which I have suggested, a spirit of forbearance and self-respect had been cherished which rendered their intercourse with each other pleasant, and, may I not hope, their connection with the School at the same time pleasant and profitable.

It seemed to me that if these habits of thought and self-discipline were carried with them into active life, they might exert a power and an influence over the opinions and feelings of others which, in this day of rash and inconsiderate action in all parts of our country, would tell upon the future of its history.

And the kind manner in which the sentiments which I had hastily sketched while following out this train of thought, were received, as well as the flattering terms in which, through you, they have been pleased to ask for their publication, are a most gratifying assurance that I did not miscalculate the motives which had actuated their conduct here, nor overestimate the value of the just and generous convictions and purposes with which they will go forth to their several scenes of active duty and usefulness.

It was, let me add, with these motives and feelings, that I prepared what I now commit to your charge.

There is another reason which leads me to yield my own judgment in the matter of its publication.

The condition of the School the present year, unless it may be in numbers, is not a peculiar one. What we have witnessed, the present term, of harmony and good fellowship, has been, I am assured, its normal state ever since its establishment. Those who have heretofore shared in its advantages will be able to judge from their own experience and observation whether the estimate I have in this lecture ventured to offer, of the elements of a lawyer's success, has been exaggerated or misconceived.

And I greatly mistake, or the sentiments which have been received with favor by you and those whom you represent, will find a cordial response wherever they may meet the eye of a student of Harvard Law School, and will awaken some of those pleasant memories which I trust will be among the treasured fruits of their connection with it, who during the term just closed, have placed my associates and myself under a grateful sense of their uniform diligence, courtesy and kindness.

Again thanking you and the gentlemen whom you represent, with renewed sentiments of regard,

I am, very truly, your and their friend and obedient servant,

EMORY WASHBURN.

LECTURE.

Gentlemen,—

It has been customary, and there is an obvious propriety in observing the usage, to devote a portion of the closing lecture of the term, to the consideration of topics of a less technical character than those usually discussed in the lecture room.

After a period of twenty weeks, devoted to the attainment of a common object, reading the same books, discussing the same topics, and meeting, daily, on a common arena, it cannot be ill-timed or inappropriate to stop a moment, at its close, and recall the purposes to which those weeks have been dedicated, and, in the light of experience which they have furnished, to ask ourselves and each other, how far these purposes are wise, and how far they have been accomplished.

Why are we here? and why are gathered here, for use, such costly stores of learning from the days of Bracton and Fleta, to the present time? Why should young men, whose places of birth and early training have been so diverse, and whose stages of action, in after life, are to be so wide asunder from each other, come together here, as a measure of completing the training suited to the one period, and of fitting them successfully to act their parts in the other?

To one who had never reflected upon the subject, whose views were limited by the circle of his own vision, an answer to these inquiries might not readily present itself. His farm or his merchandise, his shop or his manufactory, may so engross his time and his powers, by their more immediate and palpable duties, as to leave him at a loss to understand why an ambitious, hopeful, generous-minded young man should be willing to devote months and years of patient toil in delving into the mysteries of black letter and a barbarous tongue, or in seeking to eliminate from the complicated facts and subtle distinctions of an endless variety of cases, scattered through the pages of uncounted volumes, principles which are to be applied as rules in determining the rights of men in matters arising upon the opposite side of the globe, and an hundred years after the judges who may have pronounced them had themselves been forgotten!

And yet, l think, at the end of this, though it is the first term to some of you, I shall not be misunderstood or wholly unintelligible, if I attempt to answer for you. I have watched your diligence and your progress the present term with too much interest, to doubt that a common incentive and a common motive have been urging you on, and that this would be found in the ambition and hope of taking an honorable rank in the profession of a lawyer. I have a right to believe, too, from the same evidence, that you have had something, at least, of a proper appreciation of what it is, and what it requires, in order to be such a lawyer, as I have supposed. Nor have I any doubt you will listen to me with indulgence while I attempt, briefly, to show what are some of the qualifications it demands in order to succeed, as well as what are the elements which are involved in his success, and what he owes, in return, for whatever of eminence he may thereby attain.

In this social organization, in which we find ourselves placed by Providence, we cannot but remark that every man has several parts to perform, and each, often, apparently distinct from the other. The duties of the child differ from those of the adult, and those of the man of leisure from those of the man of business. The relation of husband and parent, or guardian, may be sustained by men who never mingle in the affairs of trade or politics, or literature, or science. And as men develop and divide themselves into their respective departments of active life, each of these is often altogether distinct from another, even in respect to the ordinary rules which are applied in the direction of its affairs. The artisan may be excellent in his sphere, without understanding the first rule that regulates a brokers' board, or ever having studied the stock-jobber's catechism of moral obligation. The ship-master would be likely to make much more speed than progress if he were to undertake to play engineer to a train of cars on a railway, and a clergyman who undertakes to turn his pulpit into the platform of a caucus, generally finds that it would be better, both for his hearers and himself, if he sometimes recalled the old and homely adage, "*ne sutor, ultra crepidam.*"

And yet I would repeat, every one must, during the course of a life, act several distinct parts, each of which has its own peculiar difficulties, and requires for its guidance a tact and sagacity peculiar to itself.

You may regard these as commonplace truths, and something aside from the training for which you came here. But 1 beg you to bear with me, while I go still further aside from the ordinary track of the law and its technicalities, and remind you that this great mass which we call the People, made up, as it is, of an infinite variety of pursuits and callings and employments, in which the individual action of each seems to be so independent of all others, is, after all, guided and moulded and moved by a common sympathy and a common will, and that it is controlled and regulated by a common judgment, which is itself influenced by some strong pervading tone of thought and sentiment. And when we look at individuals, and see how few there are who have either the wish or the opportunity to originate new trains of thought, and how many there are who, from habit and indifference, are ready to adopt, as their own, the sentiments and opinions which they hear from others, it seems a mystery how those thoughts originate which shape the character and conduct of a whole people—how it is that the same nation, to-day, thinks and feels so differently from what it did half a generation ago, and how the watchword, whose mere utterance, at one period, would stir the blood of a whole nation, may, at another, be heard with derision and contempt. "Wilkes and Liberty!" could at one time rouse all England to frenzy, where, in a few short months, Wilkes had sunk so low that liberty could not save his name from being a hissing and a by-word. And such, we have cause to fear, will be the fate of our own national watch-word, once so quick to awaken a thrill in the hearts of the people, of "Union and Liberty."

But while this popular sentiment often manifests itself in paroxysms like the sudden outbursts of passion in ill-balanced and ill-regulated individual minds, it is ordinarily accessible to reason, through the same avenues by which one man approaches another when seeking to influence his judgment or his will. And, in one respect, the effort is sometimes more hopeful for correcting irregular action on the part of the public than that of individuals; for, if a state is wayward, it is never so from that perverse disposition to mischief which individuals sometimes love to indulge.

Under a free government like ours, there are various media through which the elements of thought, sentiment and opinion may reach the great brain and heart and conscience of the Body Politic, while their sources lie concealed from the public eye. And the power of influencing the secret springs of action in the popular mind is often an unconscious heritage, even to him who wields it.

I have said thus much, preliminary to the graver inquiry how far you, yourselves, are to become responsible for the character and direction of this same power of public sentiment.

Among the sources of moral power in our country, are the press, the pulpit, the school, and the force of individual minds whose training and spheres of action serve to develop and give currency to new thoughts and opinions.

In the latter class, I include the men of our own profession, and without stopping to determine where, in the order of precedence, it would stand in comparison with others, I would urge upon you the solemn conviction that upon you, and each of you, depends, in no small degree, the character of this great nation of which you form a part—for what is the character of a people but its prevailing tone of thought and feeling and sentiment. Scattered, as you are to be, into different sections of our country, with your training, with your pursuits, and the relations into which these will bring you with other minds, you cannot, if you will, help doing something to advance or retard public opinion, and stamp an impression upon public character.

I greatly mistake, or your training here has been fitting you for this very work; and when, in after life, you shall be called upon to think and act under the responsibility of a weight of character which you shall have earned for yourselves, I have no doubt you will have occasion to recall, with satisfaction, moral. and political truths, as well as rules of social life and public duty, which were suggested, if not fully developed, here.

But I recur to the proposition with which I started, that every one has several parts to act in the affairs of life. I do not propose to follow you into your social or personal duties and relations. Much as I am sure the intercourse of young gentlemen, under the restraints of courtesy and self-respect, which you cannot fail to observe under the circumstances in which you meet here, must do in training you for the higher walks of social life, it is of the *profession* as a means of your personal advancement, and of its training as a means, and its practice as an opportunity for exerting a wide and salutary influence upon the public mind, and upon the future of our national welfare, that I would say a single word.

And, first, as to the profession which you have chosen, as a means of personal success. By this I mean the means of earning a competency, of being able to rise to a condition of personal independence which every man has a right to aim at, and to feel a laudable ambition to attain. Let, me, however, caution you against setting your standard, in this respect, too high. The gains of a professional life are ordinarily in small amounts. There are few prizes drawn in that lottery; and if you are in danger of feeling disturbed at seeing your neighbor living in a better house, keeping up a better style, and exhibiting generally the outward marks of a greater wealth than yours, you had better give up your profession at once, and go into trade, or manufacturing shoes or cotton cloth, and let your brain-culture and your brain-labor stop. Less than four in a hundred, in our cities, who start to be rich by merchandise, succeed—the rest fail. And you might be of the four—though we say nothing of the chance of your falling into the other category.

But if you are content to work for a compensation that gives you a reasonable share of personal and social independence, and to feel that while you are gaining this you are earning what money cannot buy—the confidence and regard of others, and the power of making yourselves felt, you have not mistaken your profession; you are prepared to be instructed in knowing what I believe to be as well established a fact as any in moral science or human foresight, that it depends upon yourselves whether you succeed or not. It is nearly forty years since I entered that profession, without either property or patronage to start with. There was not a human being on whom I had the slightest claim for encouragement or business. The profession seemed then to be as full and crowded as it is now, without leaving a spot on which to plant one's foot without treading upon some one already there before it. Since then I have seen almost three generations of the profession pass away—for it is calculated that, upon an average, a legal generation lasts only about fifteen years; its members after that period are to be sought in other departments of business, or in the shades of voluntary or involuntary retirement. But there is scarcely a single case that I can recall where there has been a failure to succeed in it, that one might not trace the cause of this to the party himself. Indolence, inattention to business, suspicion of infidelity to his trust, or some

unfortunate idiosyncracy of temper or manner, or something often slighter than these, has kept away those who
would have employed him, or driven away those who had
already done so: while, on the other hand, the case of a
well-read, courteous, attentive and faithful young lawyer
failing of success would be found to be exceedingly rare.

The truth is, there always has been and always will be
a want felt in the community for the services of just such
lawyers as I have last described, and when the people
find one they will, in the end, employ him and pay him.

Observe the qualification I make;—in the end. I have
not lived through so many generations without having
perceived that this same People are not always accurate or
wise in their discriminations. They are sometimes taken
by a show of smartness and ability, which is little better
than impudence and cunning; and there are always
enough of litigating men in the community who can ap-
preciate and admire trick and chicanery and had rather
employ it than honest judgment and sound learning.
But these, let me assure you, are not the classes that are
certain at last to get possession of public favor, and when
they have got it to keep it.

The public, I repeat, want, and always will be ready to
employ a class of properly trained and properly educated
lawyers, in whose judgment and honest purpose they find
they may confide.

But let me say to you in all frankness, that what is a
proper training and education for one state of a community will not always answer for another.

I refer, however, chiefly, to matters of detail, and to
what constitutes the trading part of the profession. I
know no stage of a civilized community where high and
cultivated intellect would not exert an immense influence,

and which would be strengthened and extended by being united with practical wisdom and high integrity.

But the more generally knowledge is diffused in a community the more its course of business becomes regulated and systematized; and the more homogeneous it becomes in its character and social order, the less occasion there is for that class of our profession which was once pretty numerous; which occupy that region of equivocal jurisdiction which lies between the elevated and healthy field of honorable professional duty and that pestilent morass in which pettifogging grows the rifest. Within my recollection a whole class of "collecting lawyers" who earned handsome livelihoods by an honorable practice of the law, as it then prevailed, have disappeared. The course of business in the community has rendered their services unnecessary, while a more important and complicated class of cases have been coming in to take the place of the mere collection of debts, and these require a higher preparation, and a far more systematic course of study, than was formerly thought necessary to a lawyer's success.

The requisites for this success have been becoming more numerous and of a higher order every year, till a mere uneducated writ-maker has no right any longer to hope to rise in this profession even to mediocrity. And what is now true of the older States is becoming equally so in the newer ones, till they who would share the honors of the Law must be able to win their own spurs in the field of manly and knightly encounter.

But I wish, here, most emphatically, to remind you of the difference there is, in accomplishing this, between what we call genius, and common sense united with industry. Every-body is dazzled and delighted by ex-

hibitions of true eloquence. It is a wonderful power,—
one of the greatest and most enviable that a human being can possess. But it is rarely called for in the ordinary
business of a court. I mean that display of oratorical
powers which the world calls eloquence. In not a few
of the causes which one has to manage in court, such a
display would be as misplaced as to go out with a piece
of field ordnance to attack a skulking fox, that had been
poaching in one's poultry yard. And in ninety-nine cases
out of a hundred, mere rhetoric, however rich in language
or beautiful in figure, in arguing a case to a jury, is not
only lost, but hurts a cause. You may in that way
entertain and interest a jury, but you do not convince
them. They forget your client and his cause, while they
listen to you, and you, generally, would have the satisfaction of having amused the spectators, at the expense
of your client. And this, let me assure you, will not
pay. A court-house is a place, of all others, for work,
and hard work, too. The court sits there to do its business. The jury sit there, really, to hear and decide the
cases that come before them, as they ought to be. They
want you, when you talk to them about your case, to
explain it—to show them what the real merits of it are,
and as long as you do that, and they see you are trying
to display the merits of your case instead of yourself,
they will listen to you, attentively, and give your argument its fair weight. You must to this end study your
case in all its bearings. You must understand the law
it involves, and, if you know the facts and the law, you
need not be afraid that you cannot find words in which
to frame your address to the court or jury. If to all
this industry and application, one can bring eloquence, as
well as learning, and with it, discretion how and when

to use it, it gives him a most enviable power. But where one rhetorician succeeds at the bar, ten fail. It is the race of the hare and the tortoise over again. The slow, plodding, straight-forward industry of the one leaves the other with all his fleetness behind. Those lawyers, either in England or this country, who have worked their way up into the higher walks of the profession, to places of judges or leaders of the bar, have rarely been men like Erskine, or Curran, or Pinkney, distinguished for either grace of manner, or beauty of style or language. One of the most effective, if not the greatest manager of causes before a jury that we have had in New England, made use of as few of the graces of rhetoric as could well be consistent with a wonderful clearness of thought, and an equally remarkable command of just the right words—often vernacular and of the commonest kind—to express what he thought and what he knew. And I always thought the remarkable success of Mr. Choate was far less in that gorgeous and brilliant use of language, and figure, and that captivating display of the arts of rhetoric which every-body admired, than in that never-failing, never-tiring current of sound logic which ran along beneath this exhibition of power and beauty, and carried a jury by the force of conviction. His was not the idle play of a brilliant fancy, but the utterance of deliberate thought, elaborately wrought out, though clothed in language of unsurpassed affluence and beauty.

Now I say this for your caution, as well as your encouragement. All of you can work, all of you can apply yourselves, all of you can make yourselves masters of your causes, and if you cannot be Ciceros, you can talk like yourselves, and, in nine cases out of ten, you would in so doing, talk to better effect for your success

as lawyers, than if you brought to your cause the eloquence of the most fascinating stump-orator who ever
delighted a caucus.

It is hardly necessary to say that it is to fit young
men for the varied duties of a lawyer's life, in its severer
aspect, that this and similar schools are designed. The
training which is here adopted, if followed out, can hardly
fail to achieve, for one who is ambitious to deserve it, a
position of eminence and influence at the bar. The
learning that you find in these books, the hints and illus-
trations you gather from these lectures, the quickening,
stimulating process of social discussion, which you encounter here in your intercourse one with another, and
the training of unsurpassed utility which is supplied here
through the medium of Moot Courts, furnish the elements
and means of preparatory progress, which only needs to
be diligently pursued while here, and faithfully followed out
when you shall come to the bar, to ensure you a good degree of professional success. The public need the services
of just such men as such a training can hardly fail to
make you. And it matters little where the field may be
in which you plant yourselves, be it in the old States or
the new, in the commercial city or some thriving region
of the interior, if you enter and pursue the profession
with as high purposes and as diligent application as you
have manifested in your course here, I have little fear in
pledging for you the rewards which a high and noble
profession offers to its votaries who are willing to deserve
them.

But I pass from considering the profession which you
have chosen, as a means of individual success, to its far
wider and higher prerogative of influencing and con-
trolling public sentiment and opinion, and thereby of

forming and fashioning public character. I would not, while speaking of it in this light, undertake to measure the extent of its power, as compared with the other causes to which I have before alluded. And it is only because you, and each of you, are to contribute to this power, as an incident to the parts which you are fitting yourselves to act, that I again refer to its character and its importance.

In a busy, restless community like ours, somebody has to do the thinking, whose whole time and energies are not engrossed by the drudgery and details of physical labor, or the eager pursuit of the means of competence or comfort. I mean by thinking, not what each man does within his own particular sphere, but that process of examining and testing by safe and reliable standards the notions and theories and speculations affecting the broader interests of the race, which are constantly springing up, in every free community.

Notions, the wildest and most extravagant, are constantly struggling to gain a lodgment in the public mind, and so long as they are dealt with only by men who have but a single line of thought, and have never been trained to scrutinize questions as having two sides to them, they often assume for the time being, a weight and importance which sink into insignificance the moment such a test is applied.

For the last thirty years, the public mind seems to have been constantly growing more and more ready to take up these opinions upon every thing, however grave, whether philosophy, morals, or politics.

The issues to which that period have given rise, have indeed been legions;—so susceptible has the public sense been to any thing new and startling.

3

18

These, one after the other, have each had its day, to give place, in turn, to something new. Fourierism lives only in history. Mesmerism has gone up or gone down, into Spiritualism, while Mormonism finds its proper sphere remote from regions illuminated by the light of the Christian religion or human learning.

Now, during these changes and fluctuations of form, in which the several movements of the public mind have been exhibited, something has been at work, as a drag upon its extravagance, correcting its judgments and separating the true elements of human progress, from the false and pernicious speculations of men with bad hearts, or perverted intellects. I do not undertake to say how much of this has been done by one agency, or how much by another; but I have no hesitation in saying that in its accomplishment, the men of our profession have in one way and another, borne a most important part.

I have no hesitation in saying that upon you, collectively and individually, will, hereafter, devolve a most solemn duty, in aiding to control the current of public thought. Your training here, and the exercise and fuller development hereafter, of the habits of investigating the causes of what you witness, of measuring and testing the weight and force of evidence, of caution in taking any thing upon mere hearsay and tradition, and of embodying and presenting to others the results of your own examinations, cannot fail, whether you intend it or not, or whether you are conscious of it or not, to be felt upon the judgments and opinions of those around you.

It is a solemn responsibility, to be helping to shape and form the future character of the community in which one lives. And if ever this was true, it was never more so than at the present moment. Every thing seems to

be unsettled and unhinged. The public mind has lost
its balance, and the moral sense of the community has
lost its tone. Things that we were once taught to regard as sacred, are now trodden under foot as worthless.
And memories the most hallowed, and associations the
most precious and inspiriting, are made the things of
scorn and bitter invective. It is a sad and gloomy hour ;
and we involuntarily look around to see from what quar-
ter, in the wisdom of Providence, relief is to come.
Come it must, or this glorious country of ours, with all
its memories and all its hopes, is to be broken into pieces,
and the brotherhood of success is to give place to the
alienage of mutual wrong and bitterness and disaster.

That it is to come from abroad, we have no right to
hope. A free, a prosperous, and a progressive State, like
that which our country has presented to the struggling
nations of the Old World, has little claim for countenance
and sympathy from the despotic governments which have
seen their power crumbling beneath them, in the example
which our country has exhibited to their subjects and
the world. Our own government, if it is what modern
theory makes it, is too weak and powerless to stem the
current or calm the storm, in which we find ourselves
drifting upon the rocks and shoals of hopeless ruin. The
relief, if it comes at all, must come from ourselves, from
the people,—the source and element of power: not from
their hands, but from their heads and their hearts ; from
their knowledge of what is right and wise, and their
will to do it. In short, the course of public thought,
the current of public sentiment and opinion, must be
directed aright ; the dangerous dogmas which now mislead it must be exploded ; passion must be calmed, and
sober judgment and reason take the place of intemperate

zeal, and the reckless madness of the hour, or our country is to become the by-word of the pettiest tyrant of the
Old World.

If you ask me who is to do this,—who can hope to
check this flood of passion and ill blood, that is threatening to blight this fair land, I answer, you, and every
one of you, if you will but lend your hand to the work.
You have been training your minds to see that there are
two sides to every case ; that there may be earnestness of
discussion, without involving passion and bitterness of
spirit. You have been led, in the study of national and
municipal law, to trace the conditions of nations to their
true causes, and to understand that the science of government is something deeper and more profound than
the choosing of a favorite candidate for office, the shouts
of a caucus room, or the color of a cockade. You have
reflected enough to see that in the prosecution of a law-
suit between two great sections of such a nation as this,
there ought to be at least as much deliberation and sagacity brought into play, in examining principles, weigh-
ing precedents, and calculating consequences, as a shrewd
lawyer would employ in the management of a county
court cause.

I verily believe, that had the leaders in this distracted
state of the public mind but exercised half the diligence
and sagacity or honesty which you have evinced in your
endeavors to reach a right conclusion in your moot cases,
the country would have been as calm and as harmonious
as our own Law School is to-day. I verily believe that, if
you, and young men trained like you, would, even now,
bring into exercise the same processes of investigating and
enforcing what in your judgment is right and politic
and wise, which you have been doing in preparing to be

lawyers, the passions of the public might be allayed, reason might again resume its sway in the action of the people, and our country yet be saved.

The truth is, our own profession is the only one which, by training, by habit and by necessity, is able to carry on excited discussions without awaking personal passion to blind or mislead judgment. We have to do it, and we have to forget, and to see how idle is the language and intemperance of over-zeal in the management of a cause, till we are able, in the very heat of debate, however excited, to perceive and give its proper weight to the strength of our adversary's position. And with all this we are compelled, as well by the circumstances by which we are surrounded, as the force of habit thereby created, to observe the courtesies of debate which do so much to disarm controversy of its bitterness. The clergyman, on the contrary, is so accustomed to look at every thing in the light of conscience, that he tests every thing by that standard, and often fails to discriminate, in his own mind and feelings, between his own will and the dictate of what he vainly imagines is a tender and refined conscience. The press, too often, is compelled to follow in the lead of an excited popular emotion, while the mere politician is ever ready to make traffic of his own convictions of right, to reap even a transient triumph in the ill-merited honors which a confiding people are willing to bestow upon those who they believe are serving them with fidelity and zeal.

I am speaking of classes, only, in what I am saying, and while we find strong minds, honest purposes and unselfish devotion to country in every class and calling and profession into which the people are divided, I have been endeavoring to impress upon you what is due from the members of a profession situated as ours is, and trained to judge candidly, to act efficiently, and to make itself felt upon a community through which it is scattered.

You will do us the justice to say that we have never spoken of sect, or party, or section, in the connection in which we have stood to you. It has been too pleasant, too personal, too hopeful, to indulge for a moment in discussions so ill-timed and inappropriate to our duties here, and the memories we would cherish hereafter.

I would not depart from this rule in the slightest degree, on this occasion. But no one can look upon this agitation, this crimination and recrimination, this readiness to rush on to untried difficulties and dangers, while our country is forgotten, without seeing that there is wrong somewhere; somebody is and has been to blame in stirring up strife among a people with a common history, a common language, a common government and a common destiny.

The mischief lies in alienated affections, perverted judgment, and inflamed passions. It lies in the public thought, opinion and sentiment. It is to be corrected, if in any way, through these. And these let me say, are directed and controlled by comparatively a small proportion of the whole body politic. The people, themselves, are honest, though often misguided. They have no interest or motive to make war upon themselves or their own institutions that are worth preserving. They only need to be shown the way of true policy and sound wisdom and they will, in the end, if left to themselves, be sure to follow in it.

And when, therefore, I ask you, in parting, to look upon our country, and to feel that, wherever you may be within her territory, you have a common country to care for, I do you no more than justice in saying that in this, as in every coming struggle she may be called to pass through, you are and you will be, by your training here, by the pursuit of an honorable and ennobling profession, by the honors you will win in its broad field, and the opportunities it will give you to fix impressions upon the public mind with which you are to come in contact, you will be, I repeat, able to do much to bring back the people to sober reason, and infuse into their minds a wiser spirit and a truer and sounder national policy.

Some of you are to enter at once upon the sphere of action, and to you the country has a right to look for a firm support of her interests and her honor. Do what you can to compel her, wherever there is injustice, to retrieve it, wherever there is wrong, to correct it. And I would say the same to those of you who are to return here for a few months longer to fit yourselves for the struggle into which you will then have to enter, if you do justice to what you and others have now a right to hope for in your career.

And let me say, in closing, that if what I have said is true of any generation of men, it is doubly so of that of which you form a part. For us who are passing off the stage it may be, personally, of little moment, whether we hereafter are to have a country or not. We have shared in the blessings of the present government, and the most prosperous nation in the world, and have been permitted to enjoy the pride which every American feels at home and abroad when he hears his country spoken of as the last hope of the oppressed. And if the bright visions of the future must fade away, the ruin is to fall on a coming generation. But for you the present and the future are both full of the deepest interest. You have got to share in the good or evil which these are to bring with them, whether you will or not. And if you but will it, there is not one of you so humble that you may not do something to promote the good and avert the evil that hangs over us.

I may have wearied your patience in these desultory remarks, but my heart was too full of the issue that is before us, of the gloom that hangs over our common country, and the need there is of young, strong-hearted, hopeful, honest minds, unfettered by prejudices and uncorrupted by political selfishness, as I believe yours to be, to suffer me to keep silent on this last occasion when I shall meet you all together on this side of life's ebbing tide.

And I cannot better do justice to the feelings of my associates and myself, on this occasion, than by closing the services of the term by wishing you the best rewards which a kind Providence and a *united* and happy country can shower upon you, wherever in this wide land you may find happy and prosperous homes.

www.ingramcontent.com/pod-product-compliance
Lightning Source LLC
Chambersburg PA
CBHW032046090426
42733CB00030B/713